The Roland Bixler Story:

In His Own Words as Told to Ian Skoggard

Table of Contents

Family

In the beginning...

I was born near the town of Bluffton, Ohio. My parents were both from Wayne

County, which is in the east-central part of Ohio. This is excellent farm country and also

very industrialized with the cities such as Akron, Youngstown, and Canton, nearby. My

parents were both of Swiss-German background. My mother's people lived close to

Dalton, Ohio and my father's people were close to Kidron.[1] There's a big difference in

those two worlds. They were both Mennonites, however, the more modern, progressive

branch lived around the Dalton area. Those were my mother's people. My father's people

were in the middle of the conservative branch, the so-called "Old Mennonites."

So I was born on November 17, 1913 in what is now part of the Bluffton

University Campus.[2] The campus hadn't expanded that much at the time. When I was

born, my father was teaching at the college, I read in the college paper, the *Witmarsum*,

that they had a big celebration that because I was their first child and people brought all

sorts of gifts to the chapel service and took the day off out of respect for my parents. That

was my introduction to the world!

When my father and I were first in Switzerland, my father met a man who was a

genealogist and claimed that the Bixlers originally came from Sweden around 1200.

However, my father wasn't entirely convinced and they did not continue the discussion

any further. But I think that is where the name Bixler does come from, spelt B-X-O-L at

the time and pronounced *bischel*, the German pronunciation.[3] When they came to the

---

[1] Kidron, Ohio lies in the heart of Ohio's Amish country.
[2] Bluffton University was founded in 1899 as Central Mennonite College and became Bluffton College in 1913. The name Bluffton University was adopted in 2004.
[3] According to Delbert L. Gratz (see "Bixel family" in the Global Anabaptist Mennonite Encyclopedia Online. 1953. Web. 14 March 2012. http://www.gameo.org/encyclopedia/contents/B5428.html), Bixel

United States and started applying for land, the land recorder could not speak German so some of them spelt it B-I-X-E-L and some of them B-I-X-L-E-R. When I was in Bluffton College, for example, the alumni directory had both Bixlers and Bixels. There was a famous evangelist round the turn of the century in the Los Angeles area named Aimee Semple McPherson. Her leading business manager was a fairly well-known man named Bixel. There were rumors that the monies that were collected were not all going to the right place. It is true, I guess, of many charitable organizations.

Mother

My mother, Dora C. Tschantz Bixler, was born on April 1, 1885 in Wayne County, Ohio. She died December 23, 1954 in Bluffton County, Ohio. She married David W. Bixler on September 4, 1912. Before she was married, my mother was operated on for a goiter at the Cleveland Clinic by the famous endocrinologist Dr. Krieger. The operation enabled her to live to the age of seventy-two. She was a marvelous host and was very hospitable and gracious to visitors especially missionaries and their families. Whenever someone had a financial need she was quick to respond and organize a tag sale or some other supportive event. She was the first one to take in the needy and to bring flowers and so forth in support for causes in which the family believed. She was the consummate fundraiser for charitable causes, mostly church related, but not all. One cause was Bluffton Hospital, which at that time was not tax supported, but supported by the community and the church.

(Bixler, Bichsel) is a Mennonite family name originating at Eggiwil in the Emmental, Canton of Bern, Switzerland. The word "bichsel" was a rounded adze, which was used to hollow out wooden troughs and spouts. It was likely that persons who made or used this tool were given this name during the 15th century.

Family

My mother liked to read to my sister and me. I remember we often used to impatiently wait for the mailman to bring the magazines. She would read to us out loud and because of that, and also because my father was a teacher, we became a family of wordsmiths.

Sister

I had one sibling, a sister. Her name was Mareen, for Maureen. She didn't like her middle name. She was born in Bluffton on the 19th of June, 1917 and she died in New Haven on July 13, 1994 after returning from a trip to Europe. She had ovarian cancer and only lived long enough to help us celebrate our wedding anniversary at Church of the Redeemer.

My sister had musical talent. She was the organist and choir director at the First Mennonite Church in Bluffton and was a graduate of what was called then Bluffton College. Afterwards, she spent most of her career as an assistant director at the Academy of Vocal Arts in Philadelphia, which trained opera singers.[4] She would do the auditions, which was the only way you could go to that school because tuition was based on scholarship.

She never married, however, she had friends in musical circles from around the world and knew opera people almost everywhere she went. She always had something to do with opera companies somewhere in the world. People over there would introduce her to people and places. But we were her only family, so she would spend most of her holidays with us and a little of her culture rubbed off on me. Mareen was also the organist

---

[4] The Academy of Vocal Arts (AVA) was founded in Philadelphia in 1933 by Helen Corning Warden, a prominent member of Philadelphia society. She saw the need to provide tuition-free training for talented singers many whom might not be able to afford the expense for high-quality instruction. The school is located at 1920 Spruce St. in downtown Philadelphia.

and choir director for several Episcopal Churches in the greater Philadelphia area. She became an Episcopalian, because she thought that if she is going to participate there she felt she ought to join them.

She was just a tiny person, only slightly over five feet tall. But to see her manage the huge organ, some with five and six ranks, was a memorable sight. She could hardly reach the floor pedals! She could not reach the upper ranks easily and had to inch way over there. She would flip around on that seat and everything. But she was in control! (Now Margaret also studied organ in college, as well as piano. I think she would have done very well at that, but then we moved out here.)

She was also the corporate secretary of the Branford Manufacturing Company, which is a small company that I had. We'd have board meetings and she had to take the minutes. That enabled me to pay her expenses when she came to New Haven. She was living in Philadelphia at that time. (This is insider stuff!)

When she was living here in New Haven at the Whitney Center, she attended Trinity Episcopal Church on the New Haven Green and when she died they had a special service there in her memory. She also had volunteered in the opera program of the Yale School of Music. They honored her memory too with a special program.

Father

My father was David. He was born on the 8th of March 1886. His father was D.W. Bixsel. It's a Swiss spelling and his wife was Magdalena N. Hoffstender, a good Swiss name. She died fairly young. I didn't know her. There are quite a few David Bixlers. If they had only named me David, I think I'd be the fifth. We have a son named David. My father was David W. Bixler. He was the youngest of ten children. They were all brought up in Wayne County. He had attended school in a one-room schoolhouse with eight grades in it. After that, he trained at Wooster College in Wooster, Ohio and got a state teaching certificate. From that time he always had a real interest in travel, uncommon for one who had been brought up as a farmer. He then went back to his old school and taught all eight grades. Some of the boys were much bigger than he was. (He was short as I am.) A while ago, I visited a museum in Kidron, Ohio and when I walked up to the second floor, there at the head of stairs was his picture. That area is called Sonneberg, named after an area in Switzerland, which we visited on several occasions.

Wooster College was a very well thought of institution and he went back there to teach commercial subjects, including math, and penmanship. When Bluffton College started in 1899, then called the Central Mennonite College, they asked him to head up the commercial department.

He had played baseball at college in Wooster while he was getting his teacher's license. He was a pretty good infielder, even though he was not very tall. He was a firm disciplinarian, but fair and never really got very angry except that one time in high school when I went against his wishes. I was on the high school debating team and we had a match a hundred and fifty miles away. There had been a huge sleet storm that day and he got into an argument with the coach of the debating team and forbade me to go. I said that I had an obligation to go and that was that. I also said that I did not think that it was as dangerous as he thought it was, and so I went. It was kind of the dividing line in our relationship. We never had a formal forgiveness, but eventually it got smoothed over.

My father became assistant cashier of the Commercial Bank and Trust Company in Bluffton, which was the largest bank in town. The banking then was different. You really had a banker that you could confide in. My father would do everything: advise on insurance, or taxes; clerk at an auction sale; you name it. However later they would not let him do the legal practices because the lawyers had changed the laws so that only lawyers could do those kinds of things.

My father moved up from an assistant cashier to cashier when the cashier moved up to president. The president of the bank was a man who had run for Congress and had traveled around the world. I was the janitor at that time for the bank while I was still going to high school. No secret how I got the job! The bank president owned five private banks, some of which went under in the Great Depression. There was at that time a law in a number of states called double indemnity. For instance, an assistant cashier might put some savings into purchasing bank stock so he would have a better voting position in the bank corporation. However, if you paid a hundred dollars a share for the stock, when the bank failed, you not only lost your investment, but the state banking people could come around and demand you cover the bank's losses and you end up paying double. My father did so honestly, but people found fancy excuses for not paying.

And so one night the bank examiner came by and closed the bank. I was a janitor working that night, so I heard practically the whole thing and it made a profound impression on me. I had never seen my father in tears before. He went to bed for a day and a half in tears because he thought all the people who put confidence in him and so forth would now regard him as a traitor. So he not only lost his investment, but did not have a job, either.

Apparently the state banking commissioner got word that he was a reliable person and so they offered him a job as a liquidator and conservator. At that time when banks were failing, you could take fifty percent of the assets and keep going and liquidate the other fifty percent. He was assigned to five or six banks down in southern Ohio. He would go down there Sunday night and then drive back to Bluffton Friday night. He was very successful because he was tough and very reliable. He was the only person who ever went to the state banking department in Ohio and said, "Here's my resignation. I've done all I could do. I've squeezed out all the liquidity I can. One can spend a lifetime trying to get the rest, but that's not what I want to do." It got to a point where it just cost too much to run the program.

We were middle class and headed upwards until the banks failed. The double indemnity on bank stock made it really tough. But it was not so terrible, because so many other people were in the same situation, feeling the hard times. We really did not think of ourselves as poor, because poverty was a thing we all had to cope with. Another thing that helped was we had a strong church. Although a minority denomination in our nation, we were the largest church in Bluffton. In addition there were three other Mennonite churches within two miles of what we called The Settlement. Margaret would see it kind of differently because she belonged to the Presbyterian Church and they never had quite enough members. She always thought us as the "Big Bold Mennonites over there."

When Dad came back to Bluffton in the middle of the Great Depression and they asked him to take on a nasty job of business officer at Bluffton College. He found an honorable way to save the college from going through bankruptcy. He talked to the creditors and promised them that if the college stayed in business, it would continue to be their customer for many years to come. Also the college had some bonds out and he said to those bondholders, "Look, if you do it our way, you will get forty or fifty percent of your money back, but if go through bankruptcy, the lawyers and everybody else are going to sop it all up and there will be nothing left for you." His job as business officer was really to figure out all the deals that could be made. The result was that the college did not fail. It never went through bankruptcy.

Dad next became the credit manager for the Triplett Electrical Instrument Company. He had a tough reputation. If you promised to do something he would dog you until you did it. At first the sales people thought he was a disaster, but as they got to know him, they soon trusted him and the company prospered a great deal.

Now there are a few things I especially remember about the town of Bluffton that might have an interest to the larger pubic. Bluffton is a small town of even now only four thousand people, back then maybe only two thousand. However, it became famous because the notorious John Dillinger robbed the Citizen's Nation Bank, which was a rival to the Commercial Bank and Trust Company in Bluffton.[5] I remember I ran an errand for my mother that day and drove up to Bowling Green, where Bowling Green State University is now. When I got back to Bluffton, I saw the Main Street was still in shock and the rival bank was pulling its shades down to close operations for the day. I saw the roly-poly editor of the Bluffton News roll out from under a car where he dove to miss the hail of bullets. John Dillinger was later captured and put in the Allen County jail in Lima, the county seat, which was near Bluffton. His gang came along, murdered the sheriff, and got Dillinger out. It was not until a couple of years later that Dillinger was

---

[5] John Dillinger (1903-1934) was a notorious bank robber of Depression-era United States, robbing two-dozen banks and four police stations in four states in the years 1933-34. He escaped from jail twice. J. Edgar Hoover launched the FBI in the campaign to apprehend Dillinger, which they did in a famous shootout outside the Biograph Theater in Chicago on July 22, 1934.

caught with the woman in red in Chicago and killed by the FBI. That is as close as I came to Dillinger.

Another criminal I remember was a farmer named Tom Muller who was a customer at my father's bank. Dad said you could look him right in the eye, but he was insane. He was a real goofball, but he was bright. Well he murdered his wife. I remember they searched the whole weekend, digging up everything and finally digging up an old cistern outside of Bluffton where they found the body. He was arrested and was committed to the institution for the criminally insane where he murdered another inmate. He is the first, fairly close person I knew who was criminally insane.

After the depression, my father became chairman of the congregation. He sat on every committee and was in the choir for a while. I think one reason he was chairman was because he had some knowledge of parliamentary law. Also, he'd been a schoolteacher and so leadership came naturally to him. My father blossomed as time went on. Before when he was an assistant cashier of the bank, he had to do what everybody else said and did not get a chance to show his leadership. But one of the things he did was to be the clerk at household and farm sales. He kept tract of all the sales and then settled up with everybody afterwards. My dad got to know so many people in the community.

The five Mennonites churches sponsored the Mennonite Memorial Home.[6] There was one in Dalton, Ohio and the others were around the Bluffton Swiss area. My dad had been on the founding board and was a chairman of the board for a while. I

---

[6] The Mennonite Memorial Home campus is located on a 16-acre setting in Bluffton. The campus has independent-living duplexes, assisted-living apartments, and a 92-bed skilled nursing facility, with a special emphasis on creating environments for individuals with Alzheimer's or related Dementia. A related facility, Maple Crest is an 18-acre campus located on the west side of Bluffton and designed for independent living, with duplexes, 1 and 2 bedroom independent apartments as well as assisted-living apartments.

remember they had to decide if the Home was going to be only for Mennonites or for everybody. My father prevailed to have it be for everybody. The result is that today the area has become a very nice retirement community. Now Bluffton University alumni are moving there and can attend cultural programs and athletic events and that sort of thing offered at the University.

After I was married, I went with dad on his first trip to Europe to the Mennonite World Conference.[7] You may not realize it, but there were more Mennonites around the world than there were in the United States. For example, the biggest congregation was in Amsterdam. The world conferences were held mostly in Switzerland and some in Holland. I did not attend it myself because I had some business errands to do, one of which was to buy some spring-like parts that the Swiss made particularly well.

When we came back through customs in the United States, they asked if I had anything to declare, and I pulled out of my overcoat ten thousand springs. "Here's my receipt," I said. "I'm ready to pay you whatever the duty is."

Oh, I got the custom people so angry because you cannot do that in person. You have to do it through some bureaucracy and apparently they have to get a cut of it somewhere. They said, "Well, we'll just have to confiscate the whole thing."

I said, "I don't think you have the right to do that."

I think we had a big argument, but finally they let me bring them in without incurring duty. They said, "If you ever come back this way again, you're in trouble, big trouble!"

---

[7] The Mennonite World Conference (MWC) is convened approximately once every six or seven years. It was first held in Basel in 1925 to celebrate the 400th anniversary of Anabaptism. As of 2009, the MWC represents 99 Mennonite and Brethren in Christ national church conferences in 56 countries.

Family

My father was quite a history buff, partly because he was an excellent teacher. He looked into our family history and Swiss history. When we went to Switzerland, he had everything planned out. He had written to the town clerk in the village where we had records of our ancestors and saw who our relatives were. When we came to that Swiss town, they closed the school for the day to entertain "the Swiss who had gone to America." I remember the sales manager of the local watch company was very proud of the fact that he had a Buick. A Buick was really something way back in that time and he was going to take us out to show us the homestead from which our people came. It was one of those modest Swiss homes in which people live on the first floor and the hay and so forth was kept on the second floor. Part of the first floor is for the cattle and part is for humans. And so this sales manager was proudly going to drive us out to see it. He drove us along the rocky alpine roads, which unfortunately ripped out the whole bottom of the car to everyone's chagrin. Toward the end of the stay, we were entertained by the head of the watch company himself and he wanted to know if we would like to stop in for a little snack.

We said, "Well, we didn't really plan on that, but if you insist, we'll do it, but don't go to any bother."

He said, "No I'll have my housekeeper do it."

It turned out it was a four-course dinner and we just barely made the train back to Basel.

A day or two later, we were riding the Swiss train and we got on with all our luggage because we had various errands to do during our time over there. And here was a typical Swiss burger family on the train already as we got on. They were talking in

Schweizerdeutsch and they said, "Look at those ridiculous Americans carrying all that luggage and the like. I don't think they even know where the sights are to see here in Switzerland." And dad let them go on and on and on and all of a sudden he sprung the trap and spoke to them in *Schweizerdeutsch* and they all were absolutely flabbergasted. How could they have said those things! They wanted us to get off the train and go home and have something to eat. It was just a great embarrassment to them. I think my father enjoyed that more than anything else because they said to him at the end, "You can't possibly have been in America all that time. You have such a local Swiss accent that everybody thinks this is your home." He was a third generation American so they could not have paid him a greater compliment.

My father died of a heart attack following several years of diabetes. He died while conducting the sale of household goods a week prior to moving to the Mennonite Memorial Home in Bluffton.[8] He decided that he'd sell the household goods in the house and move to the Mennonite Memorial Home. It was the tenth of October, 1958.

---

[8] According to Margaret, Roland's father, David, may have had plans to move into an apartment attached to his house and not go into the Mennonite Memorial Home.

The Mennonite Church

I have been brought up in two religious traditions: one as a youngster growing up as a Mennonite and the second as a member of the United Church of Christ. I have continued to be a non-resident member to this date of the Mennonite Church and a full-fledge member of the U.C.C. During my first job out of college, I attended a number of Unitarian lectures in Toledo by a very eloquent but plainspoken minister. The Unitarians don't have so much falderal, particularly about hierarchy, which I never really understood. In addition, it had a social message that was intellectually stimulating. It was somewhat different than what I had been trained in religion as a youth.

I do not know much about the Mennonites' early history. They were strongest in Switzerland and Germany, and also in Holland, France, and Russia. But it is kind of interesting that the largest Mennonite Church in the world was in Amsterdam. They also had a strong presence in Russia along the Volga River. When the revolution in Russia occurred, they were massacred by the Communists and a number of those left and came to Bluffton, others went to Kansas and some to South Dakota and the Pacific Northwest. They had a very difficult time over there. They had been very prosperous and hard working farmers, and were quite good in the arts. However, when the revolution occurred they were brutalized. It was as bad as the Holocaust, although it has never had that much publicity. A whole family would be forced to dig a trench and they'd be lined up at the top of the trench and shot, and then other family members would have to put the dirt on over them. It was a very cruel thing.

Menno Simons (1496-1561) was the founder of the Mennonite Church. It was a believer's church with a biblical emphasis and literal interpretation of scripture. Simons was originally a Catholic priest like Martin Luther. The Mennonites have always believed in the simple life. They were called "the plain people" and emphasized modest dress. Some of the sixteen branches had special dress, you know, hoods and long skirts and that sort of thing. They were extremely hospitable, even to their enemies. If someone were trying to rob them, they would truly say, "If you need it, take it!" It is a nice principal, but pretty hard to live up to!

The first time I was in Switzerland there were a good many Mennonites who were there *en route* to the World Conference of Mennonites in Amsterdam, Holland. I met one of them once when I needed a shoeshine. He was aghast that I would do something like that because it was contrary to the scriptures, which essentially said that you lord it over someone if you have him shine your shoes! So I never did it!

Even in Switzerland, the Mennonites were persecuted by the state. The government apparently tried to take away their land and never gave them a chance to do anything. And so *ipso facto*, they said stay away from the government. It says something in the Bible about giving Caesar those things which are his and they took that to mean you have to depend on the government for protection, but outside of that, try and stay away from it. My uncle was one of the first people around to run for county commissioner or township trustee. He won and performed his duties for years. Quite a few of his neighbors did not think he ought to have anything to do with the government. He believed in peaceful living and forgiving even your enemies. But they were strongly anti-Catholic, because the Catholics were seen as enemies since the time in Switzerland.

I should say parenthetically that some of the strongest adversaries of Mennonites were fellow Mennonites, who did not believe the same way or who felt that the other people were violating their rights. For example, they used to put people who did not believe, or apostatized, onto a long paddle kind that would go out into the muddy water. They would strap the person on the paddle and dunk him or her into the water, and hold his head under until he or she drowned. And yet, you know, they were very peace-loving people, but nevertheless had strong convictions and felt they were doing God's will.

There are sixteen different branches of the Mennonite Church and they all tend to be pretty independent of each other. They range from the Amish on the very right to the most liberal General Conference of Mennonites, which is the tradition that my mother's people were in. My father's people were what you call "Old Mennonites." They were not ultra conservative but the woman still wore caps and that sort of thing. They were excellent farmers. They had large families because children were an asset in farm work. They believed in baptizing children at around the age of twelve when a person could make a rational choice. They did not feel that infant baptism was the right thing. Now they have consecration of infants asking parents to bring them up in the faith and all the rest of it, but you don't actually go through baptism until that later age. So that is the kind of religious background I came from.

My Swiss Mennonite heritage also included some people who were conscientious objectors for all or just part of their lives. Then there were people who claimed they were conscientious objectors but not based on any religious conviction, or living. The Mennonites did not think much of that. There was a famous example of someone who suddenly became a minister at the last minute and just as suddenly afterwards he was not minister anymore!

The Roland Bixler Story

My first cousin, Dick Pannebecker was the son of a missionary in China. Both his brother and sister became missionaries, too. But Dick was a conscientious objector and he worked in hospitals and mental hospitals during the war. He and his brother were part of some medical experiments by the U.S. Government. They set them adrift in the Gulf of Mexico for two weeks. The younger brother Bob Pannebecker also went to help in the restoration of China after the War. He then worked on the Yangtze River Project before he finally came back to Hawaii and went into the insurance business.

I tried to get in touch with him several times when we were going over the Pacific. He is one of only two persons in my whole family who ever got divorced. He was divorced from a lady in Pittsburgh and I just think neither of them really wanted to be married. He never remarried.

Another example of a conscientious objector was a man who became a medic during the war. His name is Art Baumgartner. He finally followed his father's career and became a banker in Indiana. He also was a lawyer and when I was very active on various boards and committees in Bluffton, he and I collaborated on quite a few things to reconcile competing positions on the board.

Another CO was one of the Smucker boys who volunteered during World War II do be a smoke jumper, fighting forest fires in the West. He was a classmate of Margaret's and eventually married Margaret's sister, Barbara Jean. She said he was the brightest person she ever knew. His father was the minister of our Mennonite church in Bluffton, Ohio. His parents were not at all happy to see him doing anything that seemed like it was helping the war. Unfortunately Dave was killed in a traffic accident shortly after the War.

The Mennonite Church

I had a first cousin also on my father's side who was a natural leader. If you could select the captain of the football team, Ed Moser would be the guy to choose. He was a captain of a B-17 bomber. Unfortunately, he and his whole crew went down and were killed in an accident before they even saw action. And then there was Dave Kleaver. He was the brightest fellow Margaret ever knew. He was a son of a Mennonite minister who was quite evangelical. To get a full college education, he enlisted in the U.S. Marines. He felt he had an obligation to defend your home country. He was a Marine pilot at Wake Island a few weeks after Pearl Harbor was bombed. He salvaged a plane out of spare parts and flew it up against the Japanese as a token of resistance. He was decorated for it. Soon afterwards, he was captured by the Japanese and kept captive for almost five years in Japan. When he was in prison, he had only one book to read and that was *Gray's Anatomy*, which he studied for years. Harvard Medical School admitted him on the basis of his knowledge. He went on to become a doctor up in Oregon. After the Vietnam War, he became a pretty strict pacifist and did not want to talk about the war and his imprisonment, whatsoever.

The Mennonites were strong on sharing and philanthropic service. At the First Mennonite Church in Bluffton the fundraising went well beyond tithing. The tithes are an expected obligation, but then you got families who I didn't think had any financial resources sign up for a thousand or fifteen hundred dollars. They had to sacrifice to do it. There was great sharing, too. If your barn burned down, all the other Mennonites would come and help you to build a new one. At Christmas, my father said it was a great thing if each of them got an orange. Instead, they worked on giving gifts for other people, something called a White Christmas.

The Roland Bixler Story

Quite a number of Mennonites became missionaries like my mother's sister and her husband, Dr. Lloyd Pannebecker, who was Bob and Dick Pannebecker's father. He had a twin brother Floyd Pennabecker, my uncle, by marriage. They found a missions school for boys in China, south of Peking. They did not have a whole lot of things, so he had to invent and make them. They did not have a printing press so he adapted one from a lot of other things they had around. The two brothers, Dr. Lloyd and my Uncle Floyd, were the last two foreign missionaries driven out of northern China by the Japanese. They had terrible stories about those times. They witnessed the Rape of Nanking. They were good letter writers and they would write a lot and I think some of those may be in the Yale in China archives. But anyhow the point of it is philanthropic service was modeled for us and expected of us.

Another characteristic was their enforcement of principle and beliefs. They had conviction and they traded conviction to the nth degree. Some branches, even the one I was brought up in, had shunning. Shunning is when you do not have any relationship whatsoever with the person who has committed a sin. You might think of it as being part of the most severe branches of the church, but it happened in the town of Bluffton. Around 1925, the undertaker, who was a member of the church, was accused of having illicit relations with a young girl in the community. The deacons met with him, declared him guilty, and threw him out of the church. They said that church people could no longer associate with him. Fortunately, for him, there were enough people who thought otherwise and continued to patronize his establishment, but he had a tough time of it.

They were also truth seekers. The motto of Bluffton College is, "the truth shall make you free." My maternal ancestors believed in higher education and my grandfather

The Mennonite Church

was the person who stood up at a church conference in 1899 and said, "Look, we've had enough talk about this having a college and all the difficulties and everything else, let's do it today!" And that's what really started the college. He was on the first board of trustees. His name is still on a plaque in College Hall. He was a man of conviction and action, and was not an easy man to deal or live with. He was an entrepreneur and if he heard something had to be done, he would make waves to get it done. He helped to start the Mutual Insurance Company, the bank in Dalton, and Bluffton College. Seeking truth, like everything else, is not always attainable. We are imperfect human beings.

Why did the Swiss immigrate to the United States and Canada in the 1800's and 1900's? I think there were three reasons. The first one is all wise men wanted to avoid lifetime military conscription. Understand that you were inducted into the Swiss army at age eighteen and you stayed until 65. The troops did not have fancy kinds of things. They had to train frequently and so that's one of the reasons why the Swiss Mennonites wanted to avoid was military conscription. The second reason was they wanted to find land on which to establish their families. And the third reason was for economic and social freedom. In Switzerland they were regarded as very hardworking and were strong conservationists. The good use of the land and resources had helped to build their society and economy. They were not looking for a handout. They just wanted a chance. And so America and Canada looked like a real opportunity—as it well turned out to be. Of course that is why they have since gone to Southeast Asia, parts of South America and Russia, although most of those were either killed or driven out.

But as I look back on the history, I think I learned the value of hard and consistent work. Partly because I was the smallest kid around and from early on found that I had to do things myself to prove that I could do them. Also I had the example of hardworking parents, who were intellectually striving. Finally, having been raised in a small college town had great advantages.

School Days

I was always a small kid and when I was in high school I got the feeling that a teacher—whom behind her back we nicknamed "Scruffy Byers"—favored the big strong kids and underappreciated what I was doing. One time she said something to me and I sassed her back, and she slapped me very hard! So I was sent off to the principal's office where I had to wait for several hours. My folks did not know about it—I never did tell them the whole story. The principal called me into his office and said I had the actions of a potential criminal and he was most disappointed in me. All I could remember at the time was that I did not know what the word "potential" meant and I was trying to find a dictionary somewhere to look it up! I did not have many other disciplinary things, but that's one that made an impression on me!

By high school, I had a voracious appetite for reading, especially about economics and the outside world. Because I attended a small high school and a small college, I had the opportunity to share information and ideas with older persons. In other words, I was kind of mentored, that might not have had happened in an ordinary small town, however, this one was kind of an extraordinary one.

Debating
My biggest activity outside of classroom was public speaking and debate, under the auspices of the National Forensic League, which was headquartered in Ripon, Wisconsin, the birthplace of the Republican Party.[1] Debating gave me confidence and maybe a little cockiness. The debate program was very important in high school at that

---

[1] The National Forensic League (NFL) is a national educational honor society established in 1925 to encourage and motivate high school students to partake and become proficient in the forensic arts of debating, public speaking, and interpretation. It held its first annual National Tournament in 1930.

time and so it was definitely one of the things that especially influenced me. I also dabbled in cross-country running and tennis, but wasn't very proficient at them. Margaret was also a debater, but we were never on the same team because there was that four-year difference in our ages.

From the public speaking, I learned parliamentary law and so in any committee meeting I could bring things to a head pretty well because I understood the rules and was able to take charge of things. This was psychologically kind of my payback for having been ignored in some other things. I did all those kinds of things just to prove that I could do them.

In the last year of high school, I entered the state contest in Ohio and won the state extemporaneous speaking championship. To prepare for the debate, they sit you down in the library where you have access to printed articles. They give you a topic and in two hours you had to have a speech ready. It helped if you had the gift of gab. It gave me more confidence and a feeling of being out in the world than almost anything else I did.

My favorite teacher in high school was a man named Harshbarger.[2] I think he was the head of speech department at Bluffton College, but he also did some teaching at Bluffton High School. From him I learned to take both sides of an argument and also do quick research. If you had a habit of reading a lot, it sure helped. Of all the various kinds of training I have had, debating by far was the most effective because you learn to think logically. You also learn to take both sides of an issue and you have to listen carefully what the opposition says and think on your feet. So instead of being a football star or

---

[2] Emmett Leroy Harshbarger (1901-1942) was an instructor of history and speech at Bluffton High School from 1925 to 1930.

something, I debated. In Bluffton, they had a number of good debaters. So it was a very stimulating period.

Summer Jobs

In the summers when I was in high school, I worked on a farm on the Dixie Highway, now Interstate 75 that goes from Detroit to Florida. A number of people were turning their homes into tourist homes and so I went out there during the summer to work in one and got all this experience working on the farms. A tourist home is like a boarding house and was a supplemental way to earn an income. In the Great Depression you tried everything you could! I did everything from butchering chickens, and preparing and serving meals, to chatting with overnight guests. One result though of that experience is I decided I never wanted to be a farmer. Also, I decided never to touch chicken again! And never have till this day!

The family who ran the tourist house had originally been from Wayne County, Ohio, but they had gone out to Oklahoma during the big land rush in 1890, when all the free land was there and staked out land. They had all kinds of hardships, bad weather, and Indians. I don't think they were fighting many Indians then, but they did have some conflicts with them. I decided then that I wanted to go into something where you use your brains instead of your brawn.

College

In college I majored in sociology, economics and then English. One of the opportunities I had at that time in Ohio was I took trips to various state institutions. For example, I visited the Ohio State Prison, the Boys' Industrial School, and the institution for the criminally insane. A lot of these places can help you in sociology, but I am afraid does not happen to students as much these days. I mean today they are kind of spoon-fed things. Back then they went out and did it. Also, we visited a number of schools.

I also became the editor of the yearbook and the editor of the newspaper in the college. That occasionally stood me in good stead later on. It also taught me a few things about being self-serving. A couple of times I should have bowed out and let somebody do it, but I was interested and so I just went ahead and took the job. One year I was elected the most popular man on campus! But it's nothing to be the big man on campus if you don't have much competition. There just weren't that many students there.

Because I was a small kid, I regarded football players as kind of different people although by the time I got to college my view changed. In fact, when Margaret and I were married, the captain of the football team at Bluffton College was my best man. The football coach at Bluffton College put me on as manager of the football team and the baseball team, because, although he was honestly interested in me, in the back of his head he also thought I controlled the press and he wanted an ally, the editor of the college newspaper, tied right into the program! One time, he had no candidates for baseball so he had me throw in practice so they might get the idea that they could make the team. I was a lousy pitcher! I was involved in everything so some things never did get quite done. Thinking back now, I could have done better, but there just was not enough time in the day!

One of the other things that was very helpful in living at home was there were four or five of us boys who would get together. I was next to the youngest. The youngest one graduated from Michigan State with a Ph.D. A lot of the time we would stroll up and down the main street, it was a good two-and-a-half-miles walk from one end to the other and back again. We would walk briskly. It was a little bit like the schools of ancient Greece where they discussed all kinds of topics and you learned from your older classmates. They were a pretty challenging group. One of them became a professor at Kent State University and another one became a minister and later, president of a college down in Mississippi during the early days of the tribulations down there.

Another one was David Kleaver. His father was an evangelistic Mennonite minister—not our minister. Margaret thinks Dave Kleaver was perhaps the brightest person she ever knew in school. He had joined the Marines and before Pearl Harbor, he was stationed out in the Pacific. In the early days of the Japanese attack, Dave flew their last combat plane against the Japanese, even though he had a Mennonite background. He was captured by the Japanese and imprisoned for five years, tortured at times. He managed somehow to get a copy of *Gray's Anatomy*. He read and learned it all and was admitted to Harvard Medical School afterwards. In addition, he was a distinguished and decorated war veteran.

Ralph Looker had been born in Romania. His father went over there, to Ploesti oil fields with Standard Oil, but he contracted some sort of disease. Over there he married a member of the Romanian royalty. I never met Ralph until he came to Ohio. I think we were together in the last year or two of high school, and then we both went to Bluffton College. He did not live on campus. We both became debaters.

In a small town, it is kind of interesting though how many people you find who really flourished in that situation. I learned a lot from walking with these four or five fellows. We would walk briskly and it did my legs good. In addition to that it so happened that all were members of the Mennonite church and so it was eclectic, I guess that is the word I should use about the discussions. I can't think of many situations where I would have been better off living in a dormitory. Those are some of the memories of Bluffton.

For a couple of summers, I worked for the Detroit YMCA place in Michigan called Camp Ohiyesa, up near Pontiac.[3] It had two weeks terms and for one of the terms, they invited the younger brothers of the kids who were there to come up. Well, the older brothers didn't give a hoot about their little brothers who were in another cabin. And so those kids were really turned loose. It was a problem. And then on top of it, most of them came from Detroit. Those kids had been through a lot in their lives and they could look you right in the eye and tell you the biggest lies. You never could depend on anything. It was just hectic to be a counselor in that situation. In addition I was supposed to run the camp newspaper and a couple of other things. So it was not a particularly pleasant experience, but a great one even so, one that helped me.

I had been the YMCA highwire cop in high school and college and in a number of other groups of that sort, as well as, some more sophisticated and conservative economic groups. I was always arguing for capitalism as I understood it and that time communism was really an actual threat in the schools. I later had a friend who worked in Washington at the time, and he showed me some of the files how the communists really had planned to take over.

My last year at Bluffton College, I thought to myself, "Wait a minute, the depression is really on. I've got to have something here that I can try to earn a living at when I get out of school; otherwise I'm going to be broke." So I decided that I better go

---

[3] Established in 1918 by the YMCA of Detroit, Camp Ohiyesa is a 300-acre day camp for children in grades K-8, located on Fish Lake, one hour north of the city.

back to teaching and get my teaching certificate. Bluffton had a very small but well thought of education department. The second half of the school year, I was assigned to teach American Government in the Bluffton high school. It was a very interesting experience. The principal thing I learned was that you had to have a lesson plan and you had better stick to it! I hated those lesson plans, but I still made it work. I was fortunate to have a group of very talented high school seniors, one of whom was Margaret. Two other people in that class were Dave Kleaver and Bob Krieder, who would later became a college president. I got to see them all close up! However, Margaret and I did not socialize at all during that time. Living at home and having to walk all those miles every day to school, and all the rest of it, I did not have tremendous amount of time for any social life. Although we never dated, I had her in mind as the right gal! At the end of two years in Bluffton she went to the University of Michigan because they had a speech program that she wanted, which Bluffton did not offer. She minored in music.

Just before graduation I began looking for a job and had an interview in a small town near Bluffton with the schools superintendent. He said to me, "We've had lots of discipline problems in the school and we are either going to hire all skilled experienced disciplinarians, or we're going to throw out the entire thing, and start all over again and try and grow an interest in learning. If we go the second route, you're our number one choice, but if we choose the first, well, you obviously haven't had any experience and you don't look like a person who could really discipline a class."

So it turned out they chose the disciplinarian route. I never got around to it, but I always intended to write him a letter and thank him for not hiring me, because I think I would have been stuck out there for some years!

The Roland Bixler Story

It was my nature to try to bring people together and have a parliamentary system, so there was some order to it. I could not beat up anybody; it really was not my nature to do so. As a matter of fact I grew up with a couple of ruffians. One of them finally wound up in the penitentiary for five or six years. He was a relative of the president of the bank that my father was waiting on retirement. The president raised him, but he was just not at the right age and sensibility to raise a kid that got into real trouble like that. One day I was up in his backyard and he had a large backyard where he set up some kind of thing you climbed. I fell off it and broke my ankle! Those are sort of the typical things that went on.

Another townie classmate I had who composed operas and did a lot of things along that line that I did not appreciate at the time. But later on, the last four or five years of his life, we corresponded about what happens after death and so forth. He had a philosophical bent that I had not quite appreciated earlier on.

First job

I worked that summer and then I got a job through a newspaper ad to become the public relations director and editor of a magazine called *The Exchange*, which was published by the National Exchange Club.[4] Exchange Clubs are sort of like the Rotary and Kiwanis Clubs, however, the Exchange Clubs are entirely in the United States, whereas the others are international. There must have been a thousand exchange clubs around the country. I had been the editor of the college newspaper and the editor of both

---

[4] The National Exchange Club is a service club whose mission is to make our communities better places to live." The first club was formed in Detroit in 1911 and the second in Toledo in 1913, where its headquarters is located. Founder Charles A. Berkey chose the name "exchange club" because he envisioned a place where like-minded individuals could exchange ideas and information about how to better serve their communities. Today there are hundreds of clubs in 30 districts and 12 regions around the country. The total number of exchange clubs today is around 700. *Exchange Today* is their quarterly magazine.

my college and high school yearbooks, so I had some knowledge and experience. Also I had been the business manager of the college baseball and football teams. So with that experience, I went down to the interview and managed to get the job as managing editor. Originally, I was supposed to do their publicity, but I became the editor of their monthly magazine.

My boss, the general secretary, was the head of the Rotary Club, too. He was an excellent letter writer. He thought it all out before he said something. He had a plan. Back then, the stenographer would make three copies, the white was used for the general purpose, the pink was for the files, and the blue was for circulation, for anyone on the staff who wanted to see it. And so I read all of my boss's correspondence very carefully. It helped sharpen my vocabulary a good deal! Some people regarded it as kind of a nuisance to get those papers on your desk, but I thought it was a pretty good learning experience. After that letter writing became fairly easy for me. The other thing about him was he had a way of singling out who had the power and moving in that direction. Also, he could take things that somebody had done and he would put a little twist in there that helped headquarters and his staff. So that's my first exposure to that kind of thing.

I was in Toledo for four years living in a hotel. I went home on weekends. Margaret was in Ann Arbor and I would go up there once in awhile or we would both go down to the Bluffton for the weekends. Also on the staff of the National Exchange Club headquarters staff was a graduate from the business school at the University of Michigan. His mother had some kind of administrative position at the university and so she got Margaret into the honors dorm across from the law school. So she had a nice place to stay.

In Toledo, I attended some special programs at the local Unitarian church and a number of other things of a civic nature that I got interested in. The Unitarians had lecture series, which I thought was a pretty rational kind of thing to do. Toledo was full of young people who were eager for all sorts of things. I also did a little work with Gallup on his rephrasing the questions in his polls and so forth.

Wedding Bells

Margaret graduated from the University of Michigan with a lifetime teaching certificate that was good in every state. They do not give those out anymore. We got married two weeks later in Bluffton. The day of the wedding was July 1, 1939. At that time, small town weddings were major social events. There were hundreds of people there! It was held out in Margaret's parents' garden. It was a very memorable event!

We sent out invitations to this long list of relatives from Wayne County, Ohio. I have fifty-one cousins on my father's side! Low and behold, the whole delegation of them came and my mother did not have enough food in the house, but she improvised and did a great job. It was the only time I ever saw my mother nonplussed. She opened up the door that morning and here were a whole bunch of my cousins that we had sent perfunctory wedding invitations to. My mother's jaw kind of fell, but it did not take long until she had things coming.

Margaret's mother had just come back from a trip with her father to the eastern coast of South America. They cruised all the way down to Terra del Fuego. It was a life-long trip that they had planned to take. It was partly business and partly pleasure for my father-in-law. Margaret's mother had to go even though she was supposed to be planning this wedding! It takes six months to plan one, you know, and they got back only a couple of weeks before our wedding day.

On the night before the wedding, I rode down from Toledo on an Interurban bus There was this big box in the aisle, which everybody stumbled over when they got on and cursed the person who was bringing that kind of luggage. It was too heavy to put up in the overhead racks, but the Interurban company would take on freight like that. And low and behold, when I got to Bluffton I was surprised to find all these ladies there to meet me. Why, were they there? Actually, they were not there to greet me, but were there to pick up the wedding cake! Well, this big box was the wedding cake that they ordered from Toledo!

Anyhow, we got through the wedding in good shape. They rented an electric organ and put it out in the garden, so my sister could provide the music. It all went pretty well except right in the middle of the wedding, just when Margaret's minister was saying something, up popped the head of a sixteen-millimeter camera and it got us all flustered. But at any rate, it was a very wonderful event!

I should also say that one of the things in my parents' home was there was always a great deal of hospitality. We had foreign visitors and people associated with the college, even though my father was not there any more. And that was a good learning experience for me. Besides hospitality, my mother was a great fundraiser. She was a very mild person but she had no fear of asking somebody for donations for anything. She could always briskly organize a tag sale for something such as the community hospital. Also, she was a fine cook.

For that summer, Margaret and I moved to faculty housing on the campus of the University of Toledo, because the faculty was gone at the time and I still had my job in Toledo. Her parents loaned us a car and we found a place to park it. About three months later I started to see about the prospects of starting a brand new company somewhere. This was at the suggestion of R.L. Triplett, Margaret's father, who was an inventor and an entrepreneur. He knew an engineer named Manfred Johnson based in Connecticut whose mission in life was to help start up electrical instrument companies. And so we made a decision to form a company. I resigned from my job at the Exchange Club in Toledo and we came East knowing only two people.

Top: Roland and Mareen; Bottom: Mareen and Roland, graduating from Bluffton College

Clockwise from top left: Father-in-Law, R. L. Triplett; Margaret; Roland and Margaret in the office at JBT; Family Christmas, clockwise from left: Robert Holt (son-in-law), Katharine, David R., Margaret, Roland, and grandson, Ryan Holt.

Early Career

I grew up in a time and place where innovation and entrepreneurship were paramount. I think today, kids don't have nearly as much interest in what makes things work, or where they come from, or how you do this or that. Today, all you have to do is just turn on the switch and there it is, air conditioning, or what have you.

My personal background was somewhat different. I was more of a generalist on the humanitarian side of things and at first did not really know much about technology. I had to learn that part and I hope they learned a little of the other side from me. Although my majors in college were philosophy, English, and sociology, I ended up making technical products, partly because I went into management and worked with other people who had the technological skills. The other thing was that I found there was a world out there that was very interesting. And so I learned by trying. Also because I took my savings out of college and was just married with a very limited budget, I had to be a force out there and be successful! All the while, the sociological and the religious influences were strong. By that I mean I tried to do things in a humane way or in a way in which I tried to see the whole picture and not just how to make these widgets.

In-laws

Margaret's mother was raised out in the farmland in Illinois where she was "Pennsylvania Dutch," but she could not go to high school because there was not any high school there. So she went to the University of Illinois for high school and then their whole undergraduate program. Many universities at that time had programs such as this because many small towns had no high schools. When she graduated, she got a job in Bluffton, Ohio, where she started the Home Economics Department at Bluffton College. There she met a local inventor and entrepreneur named Ray Triplett, who became Margaret's father.

The Tripletts, in my opinion, became the leading family in town. Ray Triplett never went beyond the eleventh grade because he did not have the opportunity. He was a self-educated man, even though he had to drop out of high school because there was no high school beyond one or two years.

One time, when he and I were going around in parts of Central America, a guard saw his name was Triplett and said, "Are you related to the Tripletts, the Hamm Radio experts." R.L. said, "Well, yes, and here's my son-in-law who's just started a new electric company." He would have been successful at anything. It was at the time when inventing was life in the Midwest.

He started a company first called Readrite Meter Works. For his first job out of school he went up to Chicago for a bit as an apprentice to learn watch making and deal with small parts. His first commercial venture was to put an amp meter or voltmeter, useful for the amateur radios, into a watchcase, like the railroad conductors used to carry around. He made a receiver that got KDKA from Pittsburgh. He was a serious student even though because of his family situation, he never had a college education. He got acquainted with Charles Kettering, who was the vice president for technology of General Motors.[1] Before that Kettering had been

---

[1] Charles Franklin Kettering (1876-1958) was an American inventor, engineer, businessman, and

a schoolteacher in Northwest Ohio. Every once in awhile, Mr. Kettering would come

down to the town of Bluffton to see R. L. to compare notes. He was very helpful in

training Margaret's two brothers, stirring their interest in things. Both boys

eventually went to the University of Cincinnati Co-op Program and became electrical

engineers and then went into the Signal Corp and after the Second World War came

back and managed the Triplett Company.[2]

The boys were destined to go into business. I thought that I might want to do

the same sort of thing and Margaret and I talked it over and said, well this is a great

opportunity, but if you succeed, everybody is going to say you had a stacked deck,

because of her father. On the other hand, if you do not succeed, people would say,

"How could you possibly blow such a good opportunity?" So, we decided we would

do it on our own. It helped that Margaret was a very talented person. I think she

would have made a good engineer, but in that time women were shoed away from

that kind of thing.

There were three reasons we came to the New York area and not stay in

Ohio. The "J" in JBT, stands for Manfred Johnson, who had been found through the

Triplett organization. Triplett had a good customer called Lewis Engineering in

Naugatuck, Connecticut. Triplett was making some of the movements that Lewis

was then adapting to measure heat and oil pressure in airplanes. Mr. Triplett

---

holder of 186 patents. He was a founder of Delco and was head of research at GM for 27 years from 1920 to 1947. His most widely used invention was the electric automobile starter, which made him very wealthy. The Memorial Sloan-Kettering Cancer Center, Kettering University, and Kettering, Ohio are all named after him.

[2] Co-op, or Cooperative Education Program, was invented at the University of Cincinnati in 1906. The first of it kind it provided students with the opportunity to alternate full-time terms of school and work in order to provide them with a solid base of experience and professional development.

sensed there was a market out here and said, "Well, if you and Johnson would like to get together, you will find that he is pretty good at helping start new ideas and new products."

One trouble was, however, he could not control his alcohol and he was quite opinionated, as many engineers are. I will say more about this later. And so we came out East, but as I say, we hardly knew any people in Connecticut. Also we just did not appreciate all the responsibilities and pressures of going it alone and the possibility of failure. Like a lot of entrepreneurs, we were just driven in that direction.

Now, as I say, Johnson was one reason to come to Connecticut. Another one was that we thought we could get some help from Yale University. However, at that time they did not give a hoot about businesses. It would have helped, I suppose, if we had a real New England background.

Another reason to move to Connecticut was the strong watch industry here. I thought we would be using a lot of small parts and also could make use of local toolmakers if needed. Another reason to move was that I decided I would like to be out of that Bluffton environment. If we were going to do this on my own, I had to go someplace where I could be on my own. In particular, I had a yearning for more education and it seemed like this area was full of opportunities to continue your education.

Finally, there was a religious reason to go. Since Margaret had been brought up a Presbyterian and I had been brought up a Mennonite, we thought that it might be better to start our roots together in a different denomination. The congregational

church did not have a hierarchy and it accommodated a lot of different beliefs. We

both felt we were socially fairly adaptable and could adjust. After that, it was

serendipity. We started going to a small congregational church in Westville by the

firehouse.[3] Mainly because it was just around the corner from where we lived and so

it was a logical choice, especially since we did not have a car. The Triplett family

loaned us one for a bit, until we got going, but in the meantime, we would ride the

streetcar downtown, walk, or bike. And when I say serendipity, we just met a lot of

friendly, helpful people. At the time Ohioans thought that all Easterners were stuck

up, you know, and hard to get to know. If you were not second or third generation

here, well, it would be the end of you. But we just did not find that, maybe because

we were not looking for it.

Next we lived in North Haven, the Hamden section of North Haven, near

Ridge Road School. There was always a mix up about the mail address because we

lived in North Haven, but the mail address was Hamden. It is out near the Millbrook

section off Whitney Avenue.

After awhile various people I met introduced me to other people and I

became a member of the Quinnipiac Club and that was good for a lot of contacts and

so forth. Because of the nature of the products we were trying to make and through

other people we met, we got interested in Grace New Haven Hospital.[4] By the end of

---

[3] The United Church of Westville is on 34 Harrison Street across form today's Mitchell Library and behind the Westville fire house. Today it is a Korean Presbyterian Church.

[4] In 1945, Grace Hospital and New Haven Hospital combined to become Grace-New Haven Hospital. Originally founded in 1826, the New Haven Hospital had always been affiliated with the medical school at Yale College. The name of the hospital changed again in 1965 to Yale-New Haven Hospital.

the war I was on the board. The biggest institutional influence in some respects was

the New Haven YMCA Junior College, which was delegated by Yale to do all this

technology cheap-seat science engineering and management. I took a few of those

courses and always had people there I could draw on and so forth. They turned out

to be very helpful contacts, not exactly Yale contacts, but then there was so much

back and forth with Yale New Haven Hospital.

At the Church of the Redeemer, I met Ellis C. Maxcy, who would become the

head of the New Haven YMCA Junior College.[5] He noticed I had audited several

courses there. Also, I would get our management team to take classes there, as well.

A couple of them wound up with two or three junior college degrees. But it was a

learning experience for me, too. His successor was Lawrence Bethel.[6] He recruited

me to be on the board of the YMCA Junior College. Bethel was hired away after a few

years by the Fashion Institute of New York, which is part of the New York State

University system. He was interested in taking ideas in management and

technology to other countries, especially those in Latin America. But I remember

the big dinner banquet at the Waldorf Astoria Hotel in New York. The whole

garment industry welcomed him to be the head of Fashion Institute of Technology,

especially the factory owners who were all Jewish. (The factory managers were all

Italian and then a lot of the workers were Puerto Rican.) But anyhow, the owners all

thought it was great to have Dr. Bethel come aboard.

[5] Dr. Maxcy led New Haven College from 1932 to 1937 and served on the University's Board of Governors from 1937 to 1985.
[6] Lawrence L. Bethel was director of the New Haven YMCA Junior College in West Haven from 1937-1953. Before that he was a lecturer in industrial administration at Yale University. Today there is a student dorm, Bethel Hall, named after him.

Early Career

There was also the Manufacturers Association of New Haven County, which was quite influential because I got to meet and associate with the heads of a lot of the small and larger businesses here, which I didn't have any fear about. If I had stopped to think about it, you know, I would have said, "Well, gee, how could a small manufacturer like me get friendly with the manager of Winchester, or Sargent, or that sort of thing," but I did.

I also made contacts through the church. As soon as the gasoline restrictions died out, we went to the Church of the Redeemer, because we then were living near Millbrook, a section of Hamden. When we later bought the house in Woodbridge, we thought at first the children would go to church in Woodbridge, but no, they were in the youth groups at Redeemer and so that is where we stayed. Later in hindsight we thought it was better not to get too ingrown in Woodbridge. Nevertheless, it was great for Margaret and the kids to be in Woodbridge and not in an urban setting, especially then as I tended to travel a good deal.

I think one of the funniest experiences that I remember is we found a space, but it was a real rough space and the former tenant would not move out on time. The brother of the Dean of the Yale Law School was in partnership with a man named Riegelson.[7] They had the Riegel Drug Company and they were going to rent us space that was still occupied by a fellow who was an upholsterer. They had the

---

[7] The transcription also has an alternative spelling, "Rickleson". The Dean of Yale Law School at the time was Charles Edward Clark (1929-39) followed by Ashbel Green Gulliver (1940-1946). Elsewhere Roland says that the partner was the uncle of a future dean of the Yale Law School. His brother, Ed Rickleson, became very high in the administration in Washington and his son became the dean of the Yale Law School." Future deans are Eugene Victor Rostow (1955-1965), Louis Heilprin Pollak (1965-1970), or Abraham Samuel Goldstein (1970-1975).

filthiest conditions you could imagine. The stuff they put in the upholstery would just turn your stomach. They practically swept the floor and put it in! I went to Jake Riegelson, the commercial brother, and I said, "When are we going to get in there?"

And he said, "Well, the man needs a little more time."

I said, "Well you have some vacant space in your office? I'm just going to move into that to help the process along!"

One day, I heard Jake Riegelson who was a wholesaler of drug products say to somebody on the phone, "Well, get a com, get a com!" Obviously the other person did not understand what he was saying, because of the real Jewish accent. He said, "Comb your hair!" And so we finally got them out of there.

I finally moved into Riegelson's office to get started and also to put pressure on him to leave, taking over the available space. At the end of six months, we had worked on a couple of things including pyrometers to put in fuel oil to measure its viscosity and volume.

Johnson was a bright man and his mission in life had been to help other instrument companies get started, but he had a bad alcohol problem, so he would get fired every so often. At that time he was the chief engineer of the Lewis Engineering Company up in Naugatuck. They were making temperature indicators for the English and French planes, because World War II had just started, although the United States was not in it at the time. After five or six months with us, we made a few things. I learned something from him and I hope I taught him some commercial business things.

Early Career

Well, one day, when we were really bearing low on money, I said to my partner Mr. Johnson, "You know, it's been almost six months and the treasury is getting very low and I haven't seen any new money. You know, you're entitled to thirty-three-and-a-third percent of the company stock, but you haven't paid a penny for yours, yet. Mr. Triplett put his third up in the beginning and I put my savings into it. How about yours?"

He said, "You mean we have to pay money for a piece of paper?"

I said, "Well that's the way it's generally done. I always thought your mission was that you wanted to finally own part of a start-up business?"

"No, no, no," he said, "Triplett has some of the money, you have some of the experience, I'll do the technical things and I want a third of the company."

I said, "No, no, that's not the way we signed up."

He said, "No, no, no, you're trying to trick me!"

So we got a Jewish lawyer who was a very sage older man and he said, "Let me handle this."

He finally said to me, "Well now it's a situation where you can completely obliterate Mr. Johnson, but my advice is to try to close it gently, so you don't leave bridges behind you. I always like to win gracefully."

He taught me a good lesson there. So we went along without Mr. Johnson for a bit and then finally made the settlement with him, a hundred thousand dollars or something.

R.L. Triplett said to me, "Well the Triplett Company owns a third of the stock and we'll leave that where it is, but you can buy it back from me when you want to and we can determine the worth of it at that time. In the meantime, we'll borrow the money to buy out Johnson's portion and you can have that."

So I'm all of a sudden signing notes to buy part of a company.

Well, imagine, here I was a liberal arts guy, now a director of a technological based company. I knew something from books about economics and bookkeeping and that sort of thing, but it really was a sink or swim thing.

Margaret's father loaned us a car for a while. So I used the car and Margaret used the streetcar to come downtown and do shopping and that sort of thing. Our food budget at that time was sixty-five cents a day for two of us. Also, she was hoping to find something in education. She could teach at least part time and help out that way. But she didn't have a graduate degree, so Yale was not interested in her.

One day, she said, "Well, I'll try to go down and meet the superintendent of schools." So, she went down there, and poor girl, he just asked her questions.

He said, "Are you married?"

She said, "Yes, my name is Mrs. Roland Bixler and I was married a few weeks ago. Here's my nationally accepted certificate and I'd like to help out doing some substitute teaching."

He said, "We don't hire married woman. It's against our policy." And then he asked her, as she was flustered getting up, "Who sent you?"

Early Career

Apparently, if you did not have the right political introduction, it was a waste of time to try to be a teacher there. So Margaret helped get our new apartment in order and so forth. She also did some things for the company at home. Her mother had worked for her father in the home too back in Bluffton. When they started Readrite Meter Works, her parents used the old kitchen table and everything else to assemble the meters that her father took out in the field to sell. That's production! You take it out, you sell it, and then you come home and make some more!

We thought New Haven would be a great place to start a business. There was at the time the New Haven Clock Company and they were used to dealing with small brass parts and so forth. So we could get help from there. We had a few little nibbles for sales. R. L. Triplett was very helpful to us, too. The Triplett Company had sales representatives in various geographical territories and they introduced us to some of them and I think partly as a favor to R. L., but partly because it sounded like we had an interesting story, they became our sales representatives. A sales representative may represent four, five, or even ten different companies, so on the same call he can get a number of leads. R. L. Triplett had a great advantage and reputation. But he was so busy by that time with French and British orders and the United States, which was also trying to buy all kinds of things preparing for the war. And so he said, "I just have to take care of all the things that are on my desk in Bluffton." But essentially he said it was sink or swim. "You know, this is your company and you make it work." And we were dumb enough to get rich from that!

The Roland Bixler Story

At that time we did not duplicate anything that Triplett did. The Lewis Engineering Company was up here in Naugatuck and they were buying meter movements from Triplett. They were then turning them into pyrometers for aircraft with manifold engines used in the British planes.[8] So Triplett had a subsidiary called Readrite Meter Works, started by R.L. Triplett way back in 1903. It made volt and amp meters and pocket watches, but also by that time, they were making test equipment for radio tubes and other kinds of electronic things. We got good hints from them and sources. Johnson also helped us. The first thing we made was a pyrometer so you could tell the temperature of oil in the tank, and then we worked on a couple of other projects. By that time Johnson was not available. But we picked up a few other helpful people and from then on we grew pretty fast. We found several technical people who were very helpful. One had a Ph.D. from the University of Southern California. We hired assemblers, mostly women who had worked in the clock industry and were used to small parts. We were the first company in New Haven to have a woman foreman. They didn't do that back then, they were too dumb to do that kind of thing, you know. Her name was Mary Goggins. I hired her personally. She is still alive today. But she's not at all in good health. She was older than I am I think by a couple years. We send her a Christmas card every year. And somebody sends it back with a real scrawl in it.

We hired various people for some kind of skills. We trained even people like bank clerks. I say we came here for the wrong reason, because Yale wasn't

[8] A pyrometer is a non-contacting device that intercepts and measures thermal radiation, a process known as pyrometry. This device can be used to determine the temperature of an object's surface.

interested in that sort of thing. But I was very interested in the Federal Government

which had some of the best known universities set up training programs, so there

would be a lot of technical people coming along. One program became the New

Haven YMCA Junior College, which had been a branch of a university up in Boston

that has a work-study program, in which you get a degree at the end of five years.[9]

So I was interested. It was a way for me to pick up some school knowledge and also

hire quite a few people. There were five thousand people attending the junior

college and finally Yale got wise and said, "Hey look, we're trying to use all our

research skills for other things and so forth. Why don't we invite the New Haven

YMCA Junior College in here and they can help us and take part of the burden off

Yale to do other things?" So, I got real interested in that part and served on the

board of the New Haven YMCA Junior College. It's now called the University of New

Haven.

Some of our employees are still friends and I still correspond with them. At

Christmas time, the Bixlers hosted the dinner at the plant and everybody was

invited. In the early days, I knew everybody and later on although I recognized

everyone who was working for us, I wasn't sure about all their names. We had a few

malcontents, but it's amazing how much friendliness there was among most of our

employees

---

[9] The University of New Haven (UNH) was founded in 1920 as the New Haven YMCA Junior College, a division of Northeastern University. The college offered instruction in business and engineering to local students. The university also owed much to Yale University for the use of its buildings and laboratories and for the assistance of its faculty and graduate students for nearly forty years.
(www.newhaven.edu/about/3928/)

Later Career

Anyway, we went on with our business and were getting a little foothold in the temperature measuring instrument business. The best product we had by far was the vibrating reed frequency meter, which was also made by James G. Biddle Company, in Philadelphia.[1] They believed in very high prices and they were unable to meet the surging demand that was coming from France and Germany. So the chief engineer of Triplett developed a much simpler way to do it, which was essentially using a magnet to activate the vibrating reed from the outside, whereas the Biddle Company used a very cumbersome structure inside. Biddle had to tell the government that they could not meet demand. This was one of the great crossroads in our company's economic history when we got a good-sized order from the Frankford Arsenal in Philadelphia.[2]

The Frankford Arsenal gave us the first order because they were assigned to make motor generator sets. That is where the first frequency meters were most used. It was difficult to start making the first few, partly because the flags would go up and down because of the vibration, so we put a coil down in it made of special magnetic material. We had to get people trained to make it. A couple of times we had manufacturing problems and had to do it again. After that we were producing two major kinds of vibrating frequency meters to put on motor generator sets. Motor generator sets were extremely important because all the anti-aircraft lights used them. To tell whether the frequency was right you looked at the meter and if the reading was vibrating sixty cycles

---

[1] Founded in 1895 and incorporated in 1936, the James G. Biddle Company, named after its founder, made and imported test equipment for the electrical industry.

[2] The Frankford Arsenal was a United States Army ammunition plant located northeast of Philadelphia. Opened in 1816 by President Madison, it was the center of U.S. military small-arms ammunition design and development until its closing 1977. During World War II, research and development expanded to cover the Army's more advanced weapon systems and employment reached 22,000. (*Wikipedia*, downloaded 12/15/10)

a second, you knew you were there and if not, you had to make adjustments to the generator.

Our work led to all kinds of variations. One time, I remember there was a branch of the federal government that wanted new parts made and so we got a contract to make some of those. We put the reeds in a circle instead of a horizontal line so it would not take up as much space. But frankly, none of those were as good as the original ones, which we still use today. If you look at a Honda home generator, you see a vibrating reed in there. People wonder what that thing dancing around in there is for?

We started to make other products as well. I went down a number of times to Wright Field, which is the Air Force headquarters for lots of things of that sort.[3] At Wright Field I got to know some of the engineers. Triplett had an engineer who was really a homespun guy, the son of a farmer. He had good technical brains like lots of farm kids do, you know, growing up with machinery. He was one of the fathers of miniaturization, which is now called micro miniaturization. He predicted that within ten years there would be all kinds of things such as microfilm, micro-engineered products and so on. He was very helpful on the line too. Soon we grew our own engineer staff and they made various contributions and got some patents, but that entrée into the vibrating reed frequency meter is the thing that set us off.

We had to build a staff. For example, we had the first woman forelady in New Haven and she was good at filing those reeds and also keeping an eye on the other people's work and training them on occasion. We also had to expand a number of times.

---

[3] Opened in 1917, the Wilbur Wright Field in Montgomery County, Ohio, was used by the U. S. Air Force to train pilots and gunners, and later became center of the Air Corps research and development and flight testing. Closed in 1963, today it is the National Museum of the United States Air Force.

Later Career

By then Triplett was getting so busy on volt and amp meters, which were also on the generator set panels. So they would subcontract to us. We took them to the adjacent building and started another production line. We had a number of failures. We would try things that did not work and finally had to face up to it and go onto the next thing.

There were only about ten or twelve manufacturers of these kinds of motor generator sets in the country. I found out there was one company out west also trying to make them. I took my first airplane flight coast to coast in early 1940 to see them. They were pretty clever engineers that made what I thought was a very sloppy product. After that I spent a lot of time also down at Fort Monmouth, New Jersey, where the Signal Corps was.[4] We got to make other kinds of products besides the ones I have mentioned, but they were all related. (They are just now getting around to closing Fort Monmouth.) It used to be the head of the Signal Corp and that's where a lot of developments came for miniaturization. We even made radiation meters used for radar testing and so forth. We were always on the look out thinking about what would happen when the war ended and what we would be making then.

We never were a high-tech company. I do not want to misrepresent that we were Hewlett Packard or anything of that sort, although Hewlett Packard did turn out to be a customer of ours later on. It was in one of those years at the New Haven YMCA College, we talked a lot about postwar plans, what we would be doing after the war was over, and how might we commercialize some of these things which we developed in the war. Now

---

[4] The mission of the Signal Corps is to provide and manage communications and information systems support for the command and control of combined arms forces. Established in 1860, its sole pre-war training facility was at Fort Monmouth, New Jersey. Multichannel FM radio relay field sets and radar were both developed at the Fort Monmouth labs. In 2005, the post was selected for closure. (*Wikipedia* 12/15/10.)

The Roland Bixler Story

I honestly believed that everybody would be flying small airplanes after the war. You know out in Bethany here there was a private airport and a man had bought it for just that reason. I took a few flying lessons until I was told that my life insurance would not be good if I died in a flying accident. We had some dreams that never materialized, of course. The government's Office of Strategic Planning would give out contracts to develop things. Here's an idea and here's a dollar. Try to do something. It couldn't always be done, but, you know, maybe you tried five or six ideas before you had a good result.

Towards the end of the war, we were also thinking a lot about how to make things more efficiently. The A. C. Gilbert Company[5] really only made tinker toys and they just mushroomed in this area. We did some subcontracting for them and for quite a few other companies. All kinds of strange requests came along and I always thought that at least one of these might be a post-war product.

The first post-war product we finally stumbled into after the war came from some of our sales representatives. We had several sales representatives, one in Denver, one in Chicago, one in Dallas, one New York and one in Boston. They each would represent five or six different products. They were sort of our antennas. They'd say, "We have a company that would like to buy this thing, we can't find it, do you want to take a look at it and see if you can make it?" And so that was our best source of ideas.

During the end of World War II, we started making military toggle switches. Our one competitor was Cutler Hammer in Milwaukee.[6] They were risk competitors and they

---

[5] Founded in 1909 in Westville, Connecticut, the A. C. Gilbert Company was a toy company, once the largest in the world, and famed maker of the Erector Set. It also made toy trains, chemistry sets, and telescopes. It went out of business in1967. (*Wikipedia* 12/15/10.)
[6] Acquired by the Eaton Company in 1978, the Cutler Hammer Company was founded in 1892 and

tried to shut us out of the market. There was still a scarce supply of military switches, so we sent out a proposal to Philadelphia and got a contract to manufacture ten thousand toggle switches. The president of Cutler Hammer wrote a personal letter to the War Department and protested that they had enough capacity and we were an unknown source who didn't understand the whole thing and should be outlawed! I beat a path down to Philadelphia to protest and they decided that we were entitled to a chance. So we made them and got passed all the red tape about getting materials and so forth. We finally got a decent contract.

After the war they realized that there was a shortage of the same kind of thing and they gave out a special kind of contract, which included a contract for capital equipment, such as a big punch presses and that sort of thing. The government would retain the ownership of that equipment for five years and then if it did not need them there was a provision that let you buy the equipment afterwards. There were times when I wish we never heard of the whole thing because there was so much red tape involved! Finally, six or eight years after the war, they sold us the equipment at a depreciated price and we were able to make good use of it. However, we did not enter into the contract for that reason. We entered into it because the government did not have enough proof sources and we thought it would be a way for us to get into something that's still related to switchboards.

And then from that we went into miniaturization which this homespun engineer in Bluffton and other engineers saw coming. They said we need much smaller toggle switches and even tinier ones for computers. Cutler Hammer was a big maker of toggle

---

specialized in the manufacturing of electric starters, speed regulators, and field rheostats.

switches but they were into so many kinds of electrical equipment that they could not really pay too much attention to that one thing. Also, they were very concerned about the Japanese competition and wanted to buy an American source. So they came to us to buy our sub-miniature switches. And so we got into a huge market with only three or four competitors. We established a good reputation in sub-miniature switches although it was just our secondary product.

There was a company, Coolidge & Kinkade (C & K), in the Boston area that was making sub-miniature switches as their principal product. We had a consultant named Don Cooper who had been a business broker and a graduate of Ohio Western University. He helped us look at a number of projects, some of which were somewhat successful. A couple of them we threw in the trashcan. I am not blaming Don for that or anything, he was supposed to be out there, and look out for us. He got acquainted with C & K and when he wound up at JBT we bought thirty percent of the business and I went on their board of directors. They were our direct competitors, although we had more designs. We thought we knew the business more. We also thought we might buy them out one day. They were probably thinking the same thing.

I learned a lot from their president Charlie Coolidge. However, his partner, a fellow named Kinkade, was much more shrewd. He grew up from nothing. I was always a little suspicious of Kinkade because he was always checking into things. I figured he thought he might try to get control of us. Finally we had to face up to it and I resigned from the board and they paid us generously with thirty percent of their business, which had grown bigger by then.

Later Career

My close associate and number two man Bill Cogger said that his business in life was to make me look good. He brought the word that Cutler Hammer wanted to buy us out so he and I did the negotiation for a period of time. Margaret and I went around the world to see other Cutler Hammer companies because they had a lot of them. We wanted to see how their other companies conducted business and what their reputation was. Remember, they tried to throw us out of buying that equipment from the government! So Margaret and I went around the world and I visited a number of CEO's who had sold out to Cutler Hammer. I would ask each of them, "If you were considering this whole thing again, how would you do it differently?"

And they would say, "Oh, gee, I think they're not very strong on this kind of control, but they're very good over here." Often in the end they would say, "They're a great company."

I said, "But how would you go about making a good deal with them?" and they would give me their ideas about it and so forth.

Bill Cogger and I negotiated with the man at Cutler Hammer for two days and came back with the deal. Newt Schenk, our attorney at Wiggin & Dana, that's the largest law firm here in New Haven, said, "How did you fellows ever do that? Cutler Hammer has a reputation for being tough bargainers." In the meantime, I sold thirty percent of it to JBT, because Bill Cogger was really a great ally. We formed another company called Branford Manufacturing Company. I sold a piece to my sister, a piece to Margaret, and also pieces to the four key men at JBT, one of whom was Bill Cogger.

Bill Cogger was a periscope repairman in World War II and they sent him out to a secret base out in the Pacific. But when he came back, he went to work for GE for two years and learned some great business methods and management skills. He married a New Haven gal and wanted to show something for his efforts. So he came all the way up from toolmaker to the number two man in the company. He was very helpful, for example, if something went wrong here at the house, you know, with the plumbing or what have you, he would find somebody to come up and fix it right away so I could spend more time on what I was supposed to be doing. So, he was invaluable. His son went to Colgate University and worked with us in the summers.

His son eventually worked for GE and was invited by them to go out to China and build the largest alkaline battery factory in the world. He would spend two weeks there, then two weeks back in the States getting squared away with headquarters and so forth. I've lost track of him. One of the hardest things I've ever done is trying to get his home address near Colgate. I had a fellow at the Church of the Redeemer named Spence Colwell, who's a real Colgate booster, and he promised me he would look up his address for me from the university directory. We called him young Bill even though by then he was maybe forty-five or fifty. His name is William Colwell, Jr. Unfortunately Spence died before he could do that.

Public Service

It seems to me that making something is a very fundamental part of society. You would like to think that you are making something that is useful and at the same time it is a business that is self-sustaining and can grow and give you rewards. However, at the time the rewards are kind of secondary until you actually get to sell the stock or buy a building or something else like that, then you have something tangible. Another thing is how you motivate people to both make and sell a product.

Later Career

Also you need to find new applications because if a business is in the technological field, you have got to expect that your product line is going to change drastically over the years. You have to shake out the bad products and place your money on the good ones, even though there's no assurance they're going to be successful. I can't tell you how many products we experimented with and somebody finally said that it is not going to work and we just quietly shoved them into the cupboard. You can get sentimentally attached to a product. Sometimes the timing is just not right and you have to let go. Otherwise, it could be bad news, especially if you have a responsibility to people and their families who depend on your business.

Finally of course there's always the need for capital. I can't think of anything in the business world that does not need capital. Business people have to be very interested in society at large. They have to support education and they have to support ethics. They also have to support the invention of new things and so forth. The arts are hooked together with business to a considerable extent, everything from museums and theatres to churches and hospitals. I always felt that people in business should either volunteer or be available for some management responsibilities in non-profit world, because presumably we know more about management than most other people. That's what we do, after all, management! Also we have a network where this person knows that person, who you can call up and ask for help.

For example, when I was on the board of Yale New Haven Hospital, we helped to develop one part of the heart and lung machine. Did I tell you that story? I can't say his name right now, but he was a doctor on staff at Yale New Haven Hospital and also the President of the American Heart Association. One day, he came to see me and said,

"We're working on a project and I wonder if you can have some of your engineers help us with it?"

I looked at myself, "Holy cow!"

He said, "We really don't know anything about this and it would take us too much time to do it. We'd be out of our depth and just look kind of foolish. Since you have accepted being on the board, I thought you might consider taking on this responsibility."

So I said, "Why don't you send a man down and see what can happen.

He said, "Well, we hired a person from Western Electric. He's the first electronic medical engineer in the United States that I know of."

And so the man came down and asked us some questions. He had designed a special kind of switch, but didn't tell us what it was for exactly. So we went ahead and made him a prototype switch. They gave us a purchase order to make a couple of those and the purchase order didn't begin to cover the cost of our time and production, but I said to myself, "Well, you know, civic duty and all that kind of stuff." So we did it and much later found it was made into something called the Heart Lung Machine and this switch was the central control for it. Work was farmed out to three or four medical centers in the country to develop various pieces of the machine and we helped develop this one for them.

About two years later, I was in the hospital for a heart operation and low and behold, they used a successor to that machine on me. Somebody said to me, "How do you feel about it now?"

I said, "Well, I cast my bread on the water and it came back cake!"

Later Career

There is a model of the prototype over at the hospital. The hospital to this day is not very anxious about giving credit to anybody who wasn't on the medical staff, but it's known that we did that part. And so I feel that it was all a human investment even though it didn't do anything for our balance sheet. But in a sense it saved my life. I guess that's something for a balance sheet!

Also I volunteered five or six times at the hospital for various blind studies, where you had to go over there for two or five days a week. I was interested in knowing what was going on in the medical frontier, but mostly I just felt that that's one way I could pay back. I couldn't go over and teach a class or invent some great thing, but I could be a willing subject for an experiment. The other thing is that I was on a ridiculous number of boards, maybe fifteen or sixteen.

Business Associations

After a few years we had established a business and things were going along
fairly well. I decided that I had to try and do something with my head and move ahead in
the world. Eventually, I was elected as a member of the Board of Directors of the
National Association of Manufacturers (NAM). So here is the head of General Electric
and here is the head of Carrier, and then here I am, running a little business trying to get
along. But I think that I learned then that there is great value to associating with people
who knew more and have achieved more than me. I saw them as mentors. I was very
active and very interested in taxes and economics and so I got to be the chairman of the
NAM Tax Committee. It might not sound like very much, but actually we were invited
down to Washington and had a personal conference with the Secretary of the Treasury.
Such things that should not happen to a kid from Connecticut!

I never quite made it to the American Stock Exchange board. I was asked by a
friend, but the company merged before that happened. Actually, I was on the board of
one company that was on the American Exchange, and was sounded out by somebody on
the New York Stock Exchange, but it didn't quite come to fruition. They did ask a
number of people if they would be willing candidates to fill vacancies but I had other
commitments at the time.

Young Presidents Organization

One of the greatest influences in my adult life was the Young Presidents
Organization (YPO), which you can only stay in until your forty-nine, then its over and
out. The graduates of that organization who had been the most active in it are then
invited into the Chief Executives Organization (CEO). I became the Chairman of the

CEO one year. Some people think CEO is a kind of a millionaires club or high-class social club. About a third of the members have inherited their wealth and position, for example, the head of Coors, or the head of Motorola, but they had to work to hold onto their positions. There were a few of them who were just playboys and just living on the money that their employees made. But another third were entrepreneurs who had started from scratch and went on to make it big and survive. And then the last third were people who got into an organization and did well and got promoted. The only requirement was that one had to be president of a company by at least the age of thirty-nine. There were a few bad apples there. I won't deny it! Sadly, there were also a number of others who were suicides. They could not face failure.

The mission of the organization was essentially to become better presidents by learning from your peers with whom you could be completely open. In some other kinds of associations you may not be inclined to tell the whole story, including your failures, as well as, your successes. At CEO there was real trust to tell both sides of the story. Also if you want to know something about a company, there usually was someone there who might be able to help you. For example, when we sold our switch division to Cutler Hammer, there was a man in CEO who had sold his business to Cutler Hammer, but he stayed with them as the president of one of their divisions. I became acquainted with him and he gave me an entrée to Cutler Hammer's operations in India, South America, and Milwaukee, which was their headquarters.

One day I asked him, "Look, if you were selling your company to them again, what would you do differently? What really counted for them? What is it that they are really interested in?"

And he told me. And I think that's one reason that Newt Schenk was so impressed with what Bill Cogger and I achieved in our negotiations with Cutler Hammer.

He said, "How'd you ever get this done, I mean it is impossible to get these concessions from that firm!" CEO is the reason for it.

Also in YPO and in CEO, but especially in YPO, you form deep friendships. We developed a thing called the University for Presidents, a course that lasted five or six days. We would have outstanding speakers and be divided into various classes by topics. One time, it was my job to introduce Norman Vincent Peale and his wife.[1] We conducted a five-day seminar at White Silver Springs in West Virginia. I was on the program committee and they gave me the job of introducing him, but he got cold feet the night before. He just did not like the format. Usually, he liked to get up and make a speech. Our seminar format was different. It consisted of four tables with six at a table. We would all discuss the topic and write down our findings. Then a group of us would finalize those findings and at the end of the evening make a report. You became well acquainted with the other people at your table. It is a procedure that is used a lot in social studies, but at that time for business people it was something new. Well, Peale did not like the notion of somebody interrupting him and asking him questions and that he might have to reveal a little more of himself. His wife did not like it either! But I will tell you that by

---

[1] Norman Vincent Peale (1898-1993) was a Methodist minister and best-selling author, his most famous book, *The Power of Positive Thinking* (1952). He opposed the candidacy of John F. Kennedy because of his Catholicism and fear that he would be under the thumb of the pope. President Clinton wrote about him, "Dr. Peale was an optimist who believed that, whatever the antagonisms and complexities of modern life brought us, anyone could prevail by approaching life with a simple sense of faith. And he served us by instilling that optimism in every Christian and every other person who came in contact with his writings or his hopeful soul. In a productive and giving life that spanned the 20th century, Dr. Peale lifted the spirits of millions and millions of people who were nourished and sustained by his example, his teaching, and his giving." (http://en.wikipedia.org/wiki/Norman_Vincent_Peale; downloaded 2/2/11)

the time we got through with it all, he and his wife were completely sold. We exchanged Christmas cards for all the rest of his life and still do with her.

One of the other great things that happened for me was although I was never the national president of the YPO, I was the chairman of the program committee for the Phoenix Meetings. They paid me by having two near full-time staff persons. We would choose the program speakers and then went around the country to visit them. As a result we had a program we thought was going to achieve a whole lot of things and make by far the most efficient use of our time. Well, it did not come out exactly like I thought it was going to be. Nevertheless, it was one of the most influential things I was ever involved in. We had it all worked out and I was pretty comfortable about it and low and behold, one of our speakers, a man from Pittsburgh, who was a hardliner business type, a just-get-it-done guy, pulled out an old shop-one speech. It wasn't right for these young guys at all and it wasn't consistent with what else we were trying to do. So we finally said, "Well, you can go ahead and give this, but we had something a different in mind." We did give him a long rebuttal. The chairman of the whole seminar told us that he had a wonderful time.

Another time, we were out in Hawaii where there lived the man who built all those cars, he built bridges so fast during World War II, and he built hotels.[2] He made cars right after the war, two brands of cars. The cars were named for him, but he built a

---

[2] Although Roland could not remember the person's name, the only one who fits this description would be Henry John Kaiser, who was living in Honolulu at that time. The following bio comes form Wikipedia: Henry John Kaiser (1882 – 1967) was an American industrialist who became known as the father of modern American shipbuilding. He established the Kaiser Shipyard, which built Liberty ships during World War II, after which he formed Kaiser Aluminum and Kaiser Steel. Kaiser organized Kaiser Permanente health care for his workers and their families. He led Kaiser-Frazer followed by Kaiser Motors, automobile companies known for the safety of their designs. Kaiser was involved in large construction projects such as civic centers and dams, and invested in real estate. With his acquired wealth, he initiated the Kaiser Family Foundation, a charitable organization.

lot of other things, ships and all that stuff. He made them very fast, but mostly he had the knack of building buildings in Honolulu and Waikiki. He built a floor a day of the hotel, and they were moving into the bottom floors before the top stories were finished. He just had it in his head, the knack of organizing and building things that way.

And so the general chairman said, "Jeez, since he is here and we had a particularly good contact with him, I'd like to invite that fellow to fill one of the program slots, or create an additional slot for him."

I said, "Well gee, we put all these building blocks together already, and I don't know if its going to quite fit."

And he said, "Well gee, the truth of the matter is, I kind of asked him already!"

And so we had him and it turned out it he was a big hit. Everybody knew of him. And as it turned out we got all the credit for the whole thing even though at first I thought it was going to be a flop.

The organization had resources on how do you build a program, how you get it done, how you gather in additional resources. They assigned a fellow named Hare—I cannot think of his first name—who was an expert on that. He and I would go off and do all these kinds of things. I had almost a year's part-time training on how to create programs for that kind of audience. Margaret was also asked to do the program, but did not go because of her strong conviction that family came first and a mother should not go away for weeks at a time when children are small and especially when the father is away also.

I am a great believer in peer learning because you have the right kind of support. Now if I am just trying to impress you, or if I am trying to claim all kinds of things that I do not really do, they will see through it right away. But, on the other hand, if you can establish good relationships, your peers will tell you things that they probably would not tell their banker or their lawyer. Although we did not see some of these people more than twice a year, they became binding friends.

It so happened that quite a few of the members owned hotels and at that time they seemed to be changing ownership all the time, I finally discovered this was because there was a clause in the federal tax law at that time on depreciation. For example, you are the owner of hotel A and I am the owner of hotel B, we sit down for lunch and we discuss a few things about it. Then we sell each other our hotels and start depreciating all over again. You held yours until a bunch depreciated in value and then you sold it to me and I could depreciate the value on the property I got from you. It is very simple, but I never knew that until I got close up. I also learned some manners and techniques because a number had some training and were polished, you know, and that sort of thing and so could not help learn something from them.

National Association of Manufacturers

Mr. Triplett was a real pioneer in the radio industry back when the Ham Radio came along. He made test measurements for radio tubes to see whether they worked and if they didn't work, what was wrong with them. For example, it might be just one of the sockets. He also had a number of inventions, for instance, the electronic measuring field instrument. He knew some of the early pioneers such as Lee De Forest, the inventor the vacuum tube, and he was friendly with Paul Galvin, founder of Motorola.[3]

---

[3] Lee De Forest (1873 – 1961) is one of the fathers of the electronic age, who invented the Audion vacuum tube that takes relatively weak signals and amplifies them, which made possible the widespread use of electronics. He had over 180 patents to his credit. Paul Galvin (1895-1959) founded the Galvin Manufacturing Corporation in 1928, which began to sell dry battery eliminators, AC radio sets, and after

Business Associations

R. L. Triplett used to take me to the annual meetings of the National Association of Manufacturers (NAM), which generally were held in New York or a resort area.[4] I got to meet a number of people there. R. L. was very shy about speaking and so he liked me to be his spokesman. One time he became quite sick and asked if I would go in his stead to the board meeting of the Radio Manufacturing Association, which later became known as the Radio Television Manufacturers Association, and then finally the Electronic Industries Association (EIA). And so he was taken suddenly ill and he asked me to present his report and it went fairly well. I was asked to be on the board and a few years later, I was asked to be the chairman of the board. And so here's a guy with a business that's doing maybe five million dollars a year in sales and I had General Electric and Farnsworth and Sprint and all those kinds of companies and I think also because I was willing to take it more seriously than some of these other guys, who would have some staff do all the work and then they would just read the report and growl about something they did not like and so forth.

So at that time, I think the EIA total corporate membership had a hundred and sixty five billion dollars of sales. Now, that is peanuts today, but at that time it was a lot. I also recruited several board members and formed some lasting friendships. One of the people I recruited for the EIA board also became the chairman of it. He went on to become the chairman of the U.S. Chamber of Commerce. I still see him on late night

---

the war, televisions. He was succeeded by his son Bob Galvin in 1959.

[4] Today the National Association of Manufacturers (NAM) is an advocacy group headquartered in Washington D.C. with 10 additional offices across the country. It is the nation's largest industrial trade association, representing small and large manufacturers in every industrial sector and in all 50 states. The NAM's stated mission is "to be the voice for all manufacturing in the United States. To inform legislators, the Administration, the media, policy influencers and the public about manufacturing's vital leadership in innovation, job opportunity, technological progress and economic security.

television every so often espousing a particular argument or point. And that is also how I got acquainted with the Galvins of Motorola. And one time we were going to try and merge EIA with its only real rival and so we used the jet of Motorola because the chairman of their board was also the vice chairman of EIA. We flew out to California to meet these guys and I had a chance to see how that side of the business works also. I thought we had them pretty well convinced to join us, but finally some of their diehard members did not want to merge because they thought they had more people out on the west coast, you know, the Hewlett Packard types and so forth.

I served on the board of NAM for fifteen or sixteen years, which was a kind of record. I always accused them of saying that I was their small business advocate. There might be a hundred and seventy-five captains of industry, there on the board.[5] I knew the president of General Electric fairly well and I knew Fred Maytag and so on. Well, I finally was elected as chairman of the taxation committee of NAM. They had a number of staff that did all the work there. The interesting thing to me was that I had three staff people under me who were all college professors and had written textbooks that I had studied at Bluffton College, Fairchild, Furniss, and Buck.[6] One of them had his Ph.D. from Princeton and through him I met the head of the economics department at Yale. And so it was a great experience for me. I learned by association and simulation, and my willingness to be a kind of a student again. I think I had the advantage coming from a

---

[5] Today, there are over 200 board members of NAM (see www.nam.org).
[6] Fred Rogers Fairchild (1877-1966) held the Knox Chair of Economics at Yale University where he also received his doctorate degree in economics in 1904. His primary field of interest was federal taxation. Along with co-authors Edgar Stevenson Furniss and Norman Sydney Buck, Fairchild wrote the two volume, *Elementary Economics* published by MacMillan in 1927. Furniss (1890-1972) was also a graduate of Yale (PhD 1918) and later dean of the Graduate School. His field of expertise included foreign exchange and labor.

very small college where we had only four or five people in the class. We had to be prepared. The professor did not wait for somebody else to bail you out.

We had all kinds of resources, including one of the men they are talking about as a successor to Alan Greenspan, who is going to retire soon from the Fed. Well, he and a man from Harvard were speakers every once in awhile. One time at lunch we had four past directors of the IRS. There was a time in my life when if you said IRS to me, first I looked blank and second I'd look scared, but these fellows and I had an eye-to-eye conversation. I walked into kind of a network and I was lucky enough not to drop the ball. Also I got into some very vigorous discussions about people who wanted changes in the tax system and those who did not and so forth. It was a real experience. I think I kind of shocked them at one of the national board meetings, when they asked me to give the noon prayer. I said in effect that we are all sinners and we have all made some mistakes, and we have been forgiven. I hoped we would have a better vision in the future. That is not quite what they expected to hear! But as I look back over it all, there were certainly all the nice parts. I certainly flunked some things too. I had a habit of undertaking bigger bite of something than there was time for. I had to rush around, and put on the pressure to get it all done, although the truth of the matter is, I learned to do things much better under pressure than if I did not have a deadline. Sometimes, I wound staying up all night and often to three o'clock in the morning. I also fell into the trap of doing the easy things first and leaving the hard ones until last, which, as you know, is not good management. You're supposed to tackle the most difficult things first and if you do not get to the other things, well, it doesn't matter.

The Roland Bixler Story

One time I was invited to appear before the Joint Committee on Taxation, which is one of the major committees in the Senate, and testify on state taxation of interstate commerce, which is still an issue forty-five years later. One of the other witnesses was then the president at GE, not the little GE, but *the* GE! He had a staff that helped him of course, but I thought he made a very good statement. His staff had collected for me samples of tax forms that a small business would be required to fill out in all the states, counties, townships, and school districts in the United States. It made a pile almost as tall as I am. And so I testified before Senator Harry Flood Byrd, who was the senior senator from Virginia. He said to me, "You mean that you got to fill out all those forms?"

And I said, "Yes, and we don't have any equipment to even separate our small sales in these various places and compute the tax and so forth. We could never get anything done."

And he said, "That's a shame!"

About two weeks later, I was in Washington staying at the hotel where Senator Byrd stayed when he was not in Virginia and, low and behold, that evening he came walking down the staircase. On impulse I said, "Senator Byrd, I don't know if you remember me, but I'm the fellow who showed you all those tax forms a couple of weeks ago, testifying on state taxation at interstate commerce."

He put his arm around my shoulder and said, "Son, we sure did give them hell didn't we!"

I also learned a good deal about how the Communists were influencing the U.S. Government at the time. A staff member of the taxation committee had to work for somebody in the Department of Commerce and he told me stories that at first I did not believe about a whole plot to infiltrate the U.S. Government. They had information about everybody who worked there and the whole intricate scheme. I never realized it, you know. He even showed me copies of documents that he kept.

On ethics and giving

I think faith helps to give you a sense of ethics and the whole if other people are doing something wrongly or rightly. There have been sins of omission on my part. I didn't do anything ostensibly bad, but when I saw something wasn't going right, I didn't always rush in and say, hey guys, straighten out here. I like to think that I did speak up on some issues and so forth. But at other times I think I maintained a discrete silence and maybe that had some impact. Sometimes I wished I could have slapped a few knuckles in order to change this or that. The other thing about faith is that I also saw wonderful examples of generosity, especially in the Mennonite Church. I mean families that I knew didn't really have much in the way of resources would give a thousand dollars to the church, or they would tithe, and that was substantial money at that time. Or they would have a White Christmas gift on top of the regular Christmas gift. White Christmas was an idea based on the story of the Magi. It really meant a gift on top of a gift. You made your gift then you made a White Christmas gift and reached in the other pocket and helped some more.

I differed with some of the people in the United Church of Christ. I don't think that the measure of your gifts is only what you give to the church. I think there are many other kinds of gifts that ought to be considered the same way. For example, I think that the church ought to be doing a lot of volunteering. I haven't done any volunteering to speak of in recent years, although I did help raise money for something like hospice in the early days. I thought of that as a religious act, but some people don't think that way. They think since the church didn't control it, it wasn't a gift. If it wasn't church related it shouldn't count as tithing.

Margaret and I have followed a philosophy in which we give to a great many things rather than giving one or two monumental, notable gifts. I think three or four years ago we were giving away well over a hundred tax-deductible gifts, but the result is you don't do a great big lot for any one body. The Mennonites have a modesty that we don't like to be thought of as the biggest giver, you know, standing out there and saying look at me, that kind of thing. But at the same time they like to do their share. As I say, I've been pleasantly surprised at various times by how much families I thought had very sparse income did give. I looked just a number of years ago at the U.C.C. Church, for example, but I think in the last few years it's pleasing to see how the level of gifts has gone up. I don't know whether it's capital gifts, or something. I think it has to be that way because I don't think there are that many members that have a potential to give. For example, the Spencer Berger Brothers was a company that made some sort of health garments and also ladies girdles and that sort of thing. Spencer Berger contributed five thousand dollars a year to the Church of the Redeemer. And that was, you know, that was big money back then. And yet he didn't attend very often.

The president of what was then the First National Bank, Chamberlain, gave very generously until one year the minister preached a sermon that castigated people who were not giving what the minister thought was enough. He left the church and went off to another church. I can think of ten or twelve instances at least where people were likewise offended.

Nevertheless, the percentage we are raising by annual gifts is not sufficient against what we're taking out of endowment. But that is kind of old fashioned thinking I have that endowments are primarily rainy day funds for capital expansion and not for everyday operations, which I think the regular church offerings ought to cover. You have got to think are we getting enough resources and also are we spending wisely. Are we getting the best return for our gifts?

Margaret and I have given to many organizations and causes and some individual things on occasions. I mean you could not get a tax deduction for it, but I was always meticulous about when we gave something that was tax deductible to be sure we kept a record of it. I mean why else would Uncle Sam and the State of Connecticut make you allowances like that? I don't think it is an incentive. Our philosophy also has been, and I'm sure many people don't agree with this, to never pledge. We say we have an intention to give, but we don't know what the future is going to hold. We are just fearful of notes or something else that can be used against us. We've never to my knowledge defaulted on an intentional gift. At least from the legal standpoint we don't make it until the last day of the year.

Obituary

Roland M. Bixler

Born in Bluffton, Ohio on Nov. 17, 1913
Departed on Aug. 30, 2008 and resided in Woodbridge, CT.

In New Haven, August 30, 2008, Roland M. Bixler of Woodbridge, husband of Margaret Triplett Bixler. He was born in Bluffton, Ohio on November 17, 1913, son of the late David W. and Dora Tschantz Bixler. Beloved father of Katharine B. Holt and her husband Robert W. Holt of Bethany and David R. Bixler of Woodbridge and grandfather of Ryan C. Holt. He was predeceased by a sister, Mareen Bixler. Roland was the President and Co-Founder of J-B-T Instruments, Inc. manufacturing electrical instruments. Active in many trade associations, he served as Chairman of the Board of the Electronic Industries Association, Board member of the National Association of Manufacturers and chairman of their Taxation Committee, testifying before the Senate Finance Committee, the House Ways and Means committee in conference with the White House and Executive Branch. He was a charter member of the Young President's Organization and the Chief Executives Forum. Roland served as a Trustee and Corporator of The Connecticut Savings Bank and helped found the former Connecticut Bank and Trust Co, serving as its President and Chairman of the Board. A graduate of Bluffton College, he served as a Trustee and later was awarded an Honorary Doctorate in 1981. From 1946 to the present, Roland was on the Board of Governors of the University of New Haven, instrumental in its transition from the former New Haven YMCA Junior College to the New Haven College, later to become the University of New Haven. He graduated from UNH with a Master's Degree in their Executive MBA program. He was awarded an Honorary Doctorate Degree in 1972. Mr. Bixler has served on many Boards of Directors, such as the Davenport - Dunbar Residence, Inc. where he was a founder, The Greater New Haven Chamber of Commerce, The Manufacturers Association of New Haven County, The New Haven YMCA, The Quinnipiac Council, BSA, The United Fund of greater New Haven, The Woodbridge Board of Education and Moderator of the Woodbridge Town Meetings. A long time active member of The Church of the Redeemer, U.C.C. he served on the Boards of Deacons and Trustees.

www.ingramcontent.com/pod-product-compliance
Lightning Source LLC
Chambersburg PA
CBHW021859170526
45157CB00005B/1883